RIDDLES &
TEASE

Best Riddles for challenging smart kids

ISBN: 9781097142804

Imprint: Independently published

Thank you for supporting our work.

https://gimbooks.info/team/rusty-cove-smith/

INTRODUCTION

I love telling jokes & thinking on difficult riddles, and I enjoy when my kids tell them to me, over the years I have collected the best ones I heard, some and old and some are fresh.

I hope this reading will give you some hours of joy as writing this book have given me. I encourage you to **"Share it with your family and friends"** an if you like it, please help me by writing a review on amazon.com

When I'm first said,

I'm quite mysterious,

But when I'm explained,

I'm nothing serious.

What am I?

The answer is RIDDLE.

Contents of the book

LEGAL NOTES

This document is geared towards providing exact and reliable information regarding the topic and issue covered. The publication is sold with the idea that the publisher is not required to render an accounting, officially permitted, or otherwise, qualified services. If advice is necessary, legal or professional, a practiced individual in the profession should be ordered.

- From a Declaration of Principles which was accepted and approved equally by a Committee of the American Bar Association and a Committee of Publishers and Associations.

The information provided herein is stated to be truthful and consistent, in that any liability, concerning inattention or otherwise, by any usage or abuse of any policies, processes, or directions contained within is the solitary and utter responsibility of the recipient reader. Under no circumstances will any legal

CHAPTER 1. EASY RIDDLES

1) What gets wetter the more it dries?

ANSWER IN PAGE 14.

2) What has a face and two hands, but no arms or legs?

ANSWER IN PAGE 15.

3) What must be broken before you can use it?

ANSWER IN PAGE 16.

4) What is so delicate that even mentioning it breaks it?

ANSWER IN PAGE 17.

5) I'm full of keys, but I can't open any door. What am I?

ANSWER IN PAGE 18.

6) What has a thumb and four fingers but is not alive?

ANSWER IN PAGE 19.

7) If I have it, I don't share it. If I share it, I don't have it. What is it?

ANSWER IN PAGE 20.

8) How many months have 28 days?

ANSWER IN PAGE 21.

9) What five-letter word becomes shorter when you add two letters to it?

ANSWER IN PAGE 22.

10) What word begins and ends with an E but only has one letter?

ANSWER IN PAGE 23.

11) What has a neck but no head?

ANSWER IN PAGE 24.

12) What type of cheese is made backward?

ANSWER IN PAGE 25.

13) What begins with T ends with T and has T in it?

ANSWER IN PAGE 26.

14) You can see me in water, but I never get wet. What am I?

ANSWER IN PAGE 27.

15) People buy me to eat, but never eat me. What am I?

ANSWER IN PAGE 28.

16) Feed me, and I live, yet give me a drink, and I die

ANSWER IN PAGE 29.

17) I'm tall when I'm young, I'm short when I'm old. What am I?

ANSWER IN PAGE 30.

18) You are my brother, but I am not your brother. Who am I?

ANSWER IN PAGE 31.

19) Which ring is square?

ANSWER IN PAGE 32.

20) I have six faces but not even one body connected, 21 eyes in total but cannot see. What am I?

ANSWER IN PAGE 33.

21) What gets whiter the dirtier it gets?

ANSWER IN PAGE 34.

22) Which word contains 26 letters but only three syllables?

ANSWER IN PAGE 35.

23) What never asks questions but is always answered. What am I?

ANSWER IN PAGE 36.

24) People need me, but they always give me away. What am I?

ANSWER IN PAGE 37.

25) What has an eye but cannot see?

ANSWER IN PAGE 38.

26) What can be opened but cannot be closed?

ANSWER IN PAGE 39.

27) What does December have that other months don't have?

ANSWER IN PAGE 40.

28) What falls often but never gets hurt?

ANSWER IN PAGE 41.

29) I appear once in summer and twice in autumn, but never in winter. What am I?

ANSWER IN PAGE 42.

30) What invention lets you look right through a wall?

ANSWER IN PAGE 43.

31) What kind of cup doesn't hold water?

ANSWER IN PAGE 44.

32) What can you catch but not throw?

Answer in page 45.

33) What makes my left hand, my right hand?

Answer in page 46.

34) What is full of holes but can still hold water?

Answer in page 47.

35) What occurs once in a minute, twice in a moment, and never in one thousand years?

Answer in page 48.

36) I'm light as a feather, yet the strongest man can't hold me for more than 5 minutes. What am I?

Answer in page 49.

37) What has teeth, but cannot chew?

Answer in page 50.

38) I can carry lots of food but cannot eat anything.

Answer in page 51.

39) What is it that you can't hold for more than a few seconds?

Answer in page 52.

40) You can eat me at night, but never in the morning. What am I?

ANSWER IN PAGE 53.

41) I'm excellent to taste, but horrible to smell. What am I?

ANSWER IN PAGE 54.

42) I have lots of money, but I need someone else to carry me around to spend it.

ANSWER IN PAGE 55.

43) What can point in every direction but can't reach the destination by itself.

ANSWER IN PAGE 56.

44) What falls down but never breaks?

ANSWER IN PAGE 57.

45) What has hands but cannot clap?

ANSWER IN PAGE 58.

46) What word is spelled wrong in every dictionary?

ANSWER IN PAGE 59.

47) Poor people have it, Rich people need it if you eat it you die. What is it?

ANSWER IN PAGE 60.

48) What belongs to you but other people use it more than you?

ANSWER IN PAGE 61.

49) Everyone has it, and no one can lose it, what is it?

ANSWER IN PAGE 62.

50) What comes down but never goes up?

ANSWER IN PAGE 63.

1) A towel.

2) A Clock

3) An Egg

4) The Silence

5) A Piano

6) A Glove

7) A secret

8) All 12 months!

9) Short

SHORTER

10) Envelope

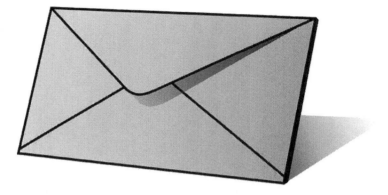

11) A bottle

12) Edam

13) A Teapot

14) A Reflection

15) Plates and cutlery

16) Fire

17) A pencil / Candle

18) I am your sister

19) A boxing ring

20) A Dice

21) A chalkboard

22) Alphabet

23) A doorbell

24) Money

25) A needle

26) An egg

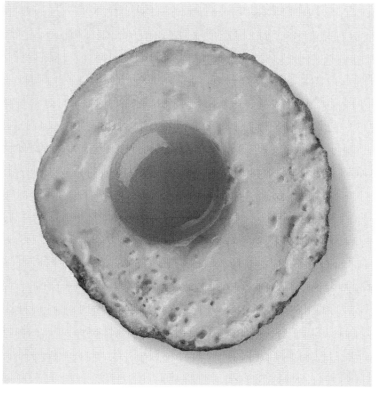

27) The letter 'D.'

28) Rain / Snow

29) The letter 'U.'

30) A window

31) Hiccup / Cupcake

32) A cold

33) A mirror

34) A sponge

35) The letter 'M.'

36) Breath

37) A comb

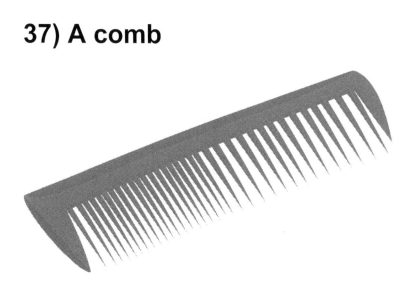

38) A refrigerator

39) Your breath

40) Dinner

41) A tongue

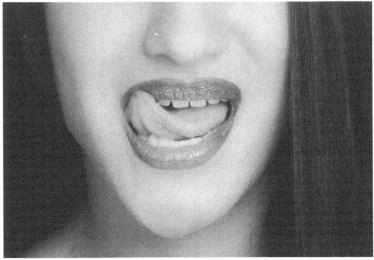

42) A wallet/purse.

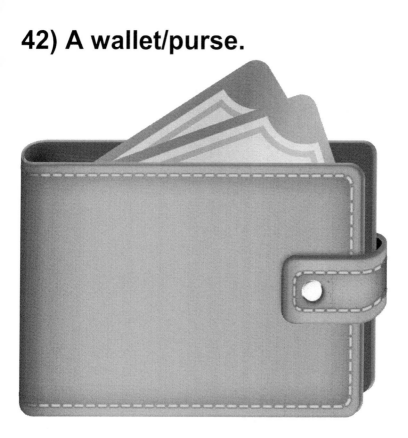

43) Your finger.

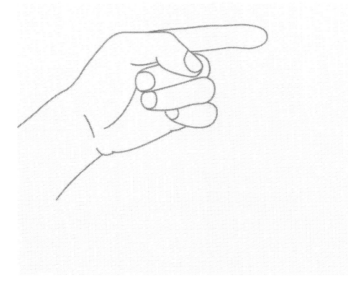

44) Nightfall

45) A Clock

46) Wrong

47) Nothing

48) Your Name

49) A Shadow

50) Rain

CHAPTER 2. WHAT AM I?

51) Take off my skin - I won't cry, but you will! What am I?

ANSWER IN PAGE 72.

52) A man shaves several times a day, yet he still has a beard. Who is this man?

ANSWER IN PAGE 73.

53) You throw away the outside and cook the inside. Then you eat the outside and throw away the inside. What did you eat?

ANSWER IN PAGE 74.

54) I have four legs, but can't walk? What am I?

ANSWER IN PAGE 75.

55) I am a ship that can be made to ride the greatest waves. I am not built by tool but built by hearts and minds. What am I?

ANSWER IN PAGE 76.

56) Many have heard me, but nobody has seen me, and I will not speak back until spoken to. What am I?

ANSWER IN PAGE 77.

57) I go in hard. I come out soft. You blow me hard. What am I?

ANSWER IN PAGE 78.

58) I am the beginning of everything, the end of time and space, the beginning of every end, and the end of every place. What am I?

ANSWER IN PAGE 79.

59) I can travel from there to here by disappearing, and here to there by reappearing. What am I?

ANSWER IN PAGE 80.

60) Two in a corner, 1 in a room, 0 in a house, but 1 in a shelter. What am I?

ANSWER IN PAGE 81.

61) I'm where yesterday follows today, and tomorrow's in the middle. What am I?

ANSWER IN PAGE 82.

62) I climb higher as I get hotter. I can never escape from my crystal cage. What am I?

ANSWER IN PAGE 83.

63) If you Run I Run, if you Stop I stop. What am I?

ANSWER IN PAGE 84.

64) I come in different shapes and sizes. Parts of me are curved; other parts are straight. You can put me anywhere you like, but there is only one right place for me. What am I?

ANSWER IN PAGE **85**.

65) I am invisible, I cannot be seen, weigh nothing, and if you put me in a barrel, it will become lighter. What am I?

ANSWER IN PAGE **86**.

66) I do not speak, but there is no word that I cannot make. What am I?

ANSWER IN PAGE **87**.

67) I am so fast you can't see me. Though everyone sees straight through me, I don't stop until the day you die. What am I?

ANSWER IN PAGE **88**.

68) I am the beginning of earth and the end of time. What am I?

ANSWER IN PAGE **89**.

69) I hide, but my head is outside. What am I?

ANSWER IN PAGE **90**.

70) I have no eyes, ears, tongue, or nose. Yet I see, hear, taste, and smell everything. What am I?

ANSWER IN PAGE 91.

71) I have four wings but cannot fly. I never laugh and never cry. On the same spot, I'm always found, toiling away with little sound. What am I?

ANSWER IN PAGE 92.

72) I am found in the sea and on land, but I do not walk or swim. I travel on foot, but I am toeless. No matter where I go, I'm never far from home. What am I?

ANSWER IN PAGE 93.

73) I am the son of your grandmother and grandfather but not your uncle. Who am I?

ANSWER IN PAGE 94.

74) There are several different kinds, but the one you pick doesn't do its job. What is it?

ANSWER IN PAGE 95.

75) My rings are not worth much, but they do tell my age. What am I?

ANSWER IN PAGE 96.

76) When I am open, I am U-shaped, but when I am closed I am V-shaped. What am I?

ANSWER IN PAGE **97**.

77) I have got three eyes, and all are in a straight line. When my red eye opens, everything freezes. What am I?

ANSWER IN PAGE **98**.

78) I'm made of wood, but can't be sawed? What am I?

ANSWER IN PAGE **99**.

79) You can easily touch me, but not see me. You can throw me out, but not away. What am I?

ANSWER IN PAGE **100**.

80) I have a thousand wheels but move I do not. Call me what I am, call me a lot. What am I?

ANSWER IN PAGE **101**.

81) He has one, and a person has two, a citizen has three and a human being has four, a personality has five, and an inhabitant of earth has six. What am I?

ANSWER IN PAGE **102**.

82) If you eat me, my sender will eat you. What am I?

ANSWER IN PAGE **103**.

83) An iron horse with a flaxen tail. The longer the horse runs, the shorter his tail becomes. What is it?

ANSWER IN PAGE 104.

84) Every night I'm told what to do, and each morning I do what I'm told. But I still don't escape your scold. What am I?

ANSWER IN PAGE 105.

85) I live where light is but die if light touches me. What am I?

ANSWER IN PAGE 106.

86) I run but have no legs. What am I?

ANSWER IN PAGE 107.

87) I live without a body, hear without ears, speak without a mouth, and being born in air. What am I?

ANSWER IN PAGE 108.

88) What is it that is deaf, dumb and blind and always tells the truth?

ANSWER IN PAGE 109.

89) I have three feet but no arms or legs. What am I?

ANSWER IN PAGE 110.

90) I fill a room but take no space. What am I?

ANSWER IN PAGE 111.

91) I have seas without water, coast without sand, towns without people, mountains without land. What am I?

ANSWER IN PAGE 112.

92) There is one in every corner and two in every room. What am I?

ANSWER IN PAGE 113.

93) I save lives on the ground and in the air. What am I?

ANSWER IN PAGE 114.

94) I shoot but never kill. What am I?

ANSWER IN PAGE 115.

95) I have a mouth on my head and eat everything. What am I?

ANSWER IN PAGE 116.

96) Tomorrow's yesterday. Yesterday's tomorrow. What is it?

ANSWER IN PAGE 117.

97) I am a fruit with seed on the outside. What am I?

ANSWER IN PAGE 118.

98) I have a hundred legs but cannot stand. I have a long neck, but no head. I cannot see, and I'm neat and tidy, as can be. What am I?

ANSWER IN PAGE 119.

99) I am a nut with a hole. What am I?

ANSWER IN PAGE 120.

100) I always have to work with something in my eye. What am I?

ANSWER IN PAGE 121.

51) An onion

52) A barber

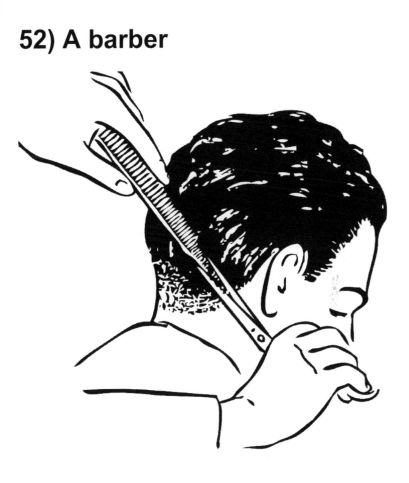

53) Corn

54) A Table

55) Friendship

56) An Echo

57) Gum

58) The letter "E."

59) The letter "T."

60) The letter "R."

61) A Dictionary

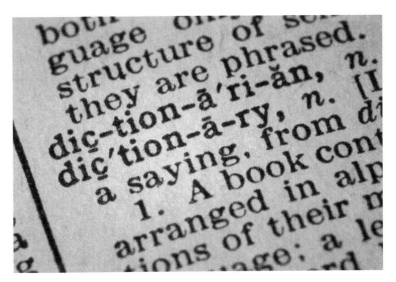

62) The Mercury in a thermometer.

63) Your Shadow

64) A Jigsaw puzzle.

65) A hole

66) The Alphabet

67) A blink of an eye.

68) The letter "E"

69) Nail

70) Brain

71) A Windmill

72) Snail

73) Your dad

74) A lock

75) A tree

76) Umbrella

77) Traffic Lights

78) Sawdust

79) Your Back

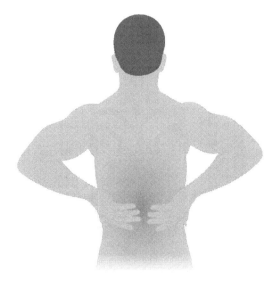

80) A parking lot or garage.

81) Syllables

82) A Fish Hook

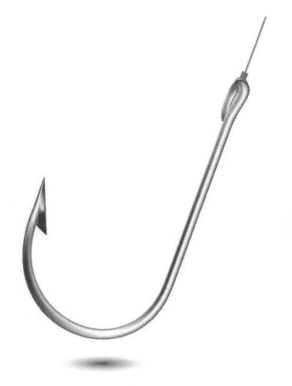

83) A needle and thread.

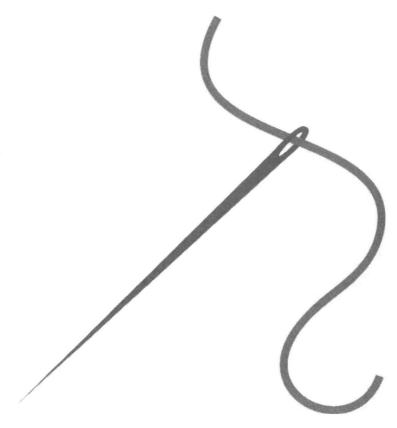

84) An alarm clock.

85) A shadow

86) Water

87) An Echo

88) A mirror

89) Yard. The length of 1 yard is 3 feet.

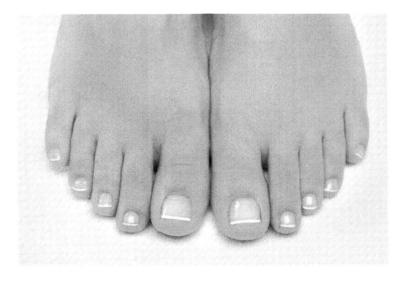

90) Light

91) A map

92) The Letter "O"

93) Seat Belt

94) Camera

95) Backpack

96) Today

TODAY IS THE DAY
to learn
SOMETHING NEW.

97) Strawberry

98) Broom

99) Donut

100) Needle

CHAPTER 3. HARD RIDDLES

101) Is always in front of you but cannot be seen?

ANSWER IN PAGE 129.

102) Take one out and scratch my head I am now black but once was red.

ANSWER IN PAGE 130.

103) A warrior amongst the flowers, He bears a thrusting sword. Able and ready to use, to guard his golden hoard.

ANSWER IN PAGE 131.

104) Come up and we go, go down, and we stay.

ANSWER IN PAGE 132.

105) First you see me in the grass dressed in yellow gay; next I am in dainty white, then I fly away. What am I?

ANSWER IN PAGE 133.

106) Forward I am heavy, backward I am not. What am I?

ANSWER IN PAGE 134.

107) Four legs up, four legs down, soft in the middle, Hard all around.

ANSWER IN PAGE 135.

108) I run, yet I have no legs. What am I?

ANSWER IN PAGE 136.

109) I work when I play and play when I work.

ANSWER IN PAGE 137.

110) I'm not more than holes tied to more holes. I'm strong as good steel, though not as stiff as a pole.

ANSWER IN PAGE 138.

111) It walks on four legs at sunrise, two legs at noon, and three legs at sunset.

ANSWER IN PAGE 139.

112) No sooner spoken than broken.

ANSWER IN PAGE 140.

113) Only two backbones and a thousand ribs.

ANSWER IN PAGE 141.

114) The man who invented it, doesn't want it. The man who bought it doesn't need it. The man who needs it doesn't know it.

ANSWER IN PAGE 142.

115) The more that there is, the less you can see.

ANSWER IN PAGE 143.

116) They come at night without being called and are lost in the day without being stolen.

ANSWER IN PAGE 144.

117) Twelve white ponies, On a red hill, Always moving, but standing still. What are we?

ANSWER IN PAGE 145.

118) What common English verb becomes its own past tense by rearranging its letters?

ANSWER IN PAGE 146.

119) What is not enough for one, Just right for two, Too much for three?

ANSWER IN PAGE 147.

120) What is seen made, but never seen after it is made?

ANSWER IN PAGE 148.

121) What kind of room has no windows or doors?

ANSWER IN PAGE 149.

122) You must keep it after giving it.

ANSWER IN PAGE 150.

123) You use a knife to slice my head, Then weep beside me when I am dead.

ANSWER IN PAGE 151.

124) What goes up and down w/o (without) moving?

ANSWER IN PAGE 152.

125) What needs an answer but doesn't ask a question?

ANSWER IN PAGE 153.

126) I am not alive, but I grow; I don't have lungs, but I need air; I don't have a mouth, but water kills me. What am I?

ANSWER IN PAGE 154.

127) A word I know, six letters it contains, remove one letter, and twelve remains. What am I?

ANSWER IN PAGE 155.

128) What question can you never answer yes to?

ANSWER IN PAGE 156.

129) I have keys but no doors, I have space but no rooms, I allow you to enter, but you are never able to leave. What am I?

ANSWER IN PAGE 157.

130) Thirty men and only two women, who have more power, are dressed in black and white, and they could fight for hours.

ANSWER IN PAGE **158**.

131) What has a head, a tail, is brown, and has no legs?

ANSWER IN PAGE **159**.

132) Can you name three consecutive days without using the words Monday, Wednesday, Friday or Saturday?

ANSWER IN PAGE **160**.

133) When does Christmas come before Thanksgiving?

ANSWER IN PAGE **161**.

134) What is black when you buy it, red when you use it, and gray when you throw it away?

ANSWER IN PAGE **162**.

135) I am taken from a mine and shut up in a wooden case, from which I am never released, and yet almost everybody uses me.

ANSWER IN PAGE **163**.

136) Before Mount Everest was discovered, what was the highest mountain on Earth?

Answer in page 164.

137) What seven letter word is spelled the same way backward and forewords?

Answer in page 165.

138) I am an odd number. Take away a letter, and I become even. What number am I?

Answer in page 166.

139) On which side do chickens have the most feathers?

Answer in page 167.

140) What is at the end of a rainbow?

Answer in page 168.

141) What flies without wings?

Answer in page 169.

142) What word looks the same upside down and backward?

Answer in page 170.

143) What goes through a door but never goes in and never comes out?

Answer in page 171.

144) What English word has three consecutive double letters?

ANSWER IN PAGE 172.

145) What is harder to catch the faster you run?

ANSWER IN PAGE 173.

146) What is it that no man ever yet did see, which never was, but always is to be?

ANSWER IN PAGE 174.

147) What 4-letter word can be written forward, backward or upside down, and can still be read from left to right?

ANSWER IN PAGE 175.

148) Why is the letter A the most like a flower?

ANSWER IN PAGE 176.

149) Mr. Smith has four daughters. Each of his daughters has a brother. How many children does Mr. Smith have?

ANSWER IN PAGE 177.

150) What can travel around the world while staying in a corner?

ANSWER IN PAGE 178.

101) The Future

102) Match

103) Bee

104) Anchor

105) Dandelion

106) Ton

107) Bed

108) Nose

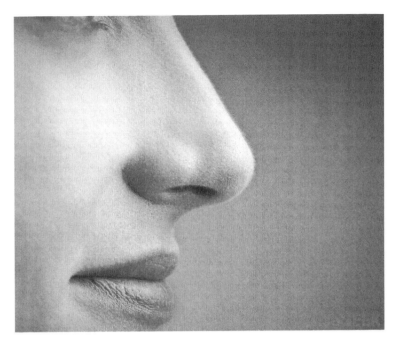

109) Musician

110) Chain

111) Man

112) Silence

113) Railroad

114) Coffin

115) Darkness

116) Stars

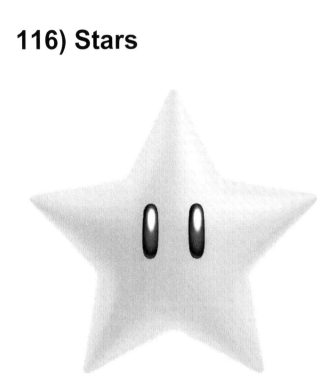

117) Teeth

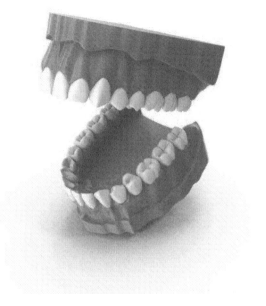

118) Eat

119) Secret

120) Sound

121) Mushroom

122) Promise

123) Onion

124) Stairs

125) Telephone

126) Fire

127) Dozens

128) Are you asleep yet?

129) A keyboard

130) Chess pieces.

131) A penny

132) Yesterday, Today, and Tomorrow.

133) In the Dictionary

134) Charcoal

135) Pencil Lead

136) Mount Everest

137) Racecar

138) Seven

139) On the outside

140) The letter W

141) Time

142) Swims

143) A keyhole

144) Bookkeeper

145) Your Breath

146) Tomorrow

147) NOON

NOON

148) Because the B is after it

**149) He has five children; all
the daughters have the
same brother.**

150) A stamp

CHAPTER 4. RIDDLE JOKES

151) Where do cows go for entertainment?

To the moo-vies!

152) Why did the elephant paint himself different colors?

So, he could hide in the crayon box!

153) What is the difference between elephants and grapes?

Grapes are purple.

154) What do you call a pig that knows karate?

A pork chop!

155) Why do bees have sticky hair?

Because they use honey combs!

156) What do you get when you cross a snowman with a vampire?

Frostbite!

157) Why did the math book look so sad?

Because it had so many problems!

158) Can a kangaroo jump higher than the Empire State Building?

Of course! The Empire State Building can't jump!

159) What did the zero say to the eight?

Nice belt!

160) Where do fish keep their money?

In the river bank!

161) Why did the chicken cross the playground?

To get to the other slide?

162) What do you call a dog that can tell time?

A watchdog!

163) What kind of shoes do ninjas wear?

Sneakers!

164) What do you call a flower that runs on electricity?

A power plant!

165) What's the tornado's favorite game?

Twister!

166)What's the difference between a piano and a fish?

You can tune a piano, but you can't tuna-fish.

167) Where do baby cows eat?

In the calf-ateria.

168)Why do sharks swim in salt water?

Because pepper water makes them sneeze!

169) Why do gorillas have big nostrils?

Because gorillas have big fingers.

170) How do you catch a bra?

With a booby trap!

171) What would bears be without bees?

Ears!

172) What's the difference between a crocodile and an alligator?

One you'll see in a while and the other you'll see later!

173) What do you call a monkey when you take it's bananas?

Furious George.

174) Why did the banana go to the doctors???

Because he wasn't peeling well

175) What did one egg say to the other egg after they told a joke?

You crack me up.

176) Why did the elephant paint his toenails red?

So he could hide in a cherry tree!

177) What do you get when you cross a tiger and a lamb?

A striped sweater!

178) Why did Darth Vader cross the road?

To get to the dark side.

179) Why do seagulls fly over the sea?

Because if they flew over the bay they would be called "Baygulls"

180) Why did the tomato blush?

Because it saw the salad dressing!

181) Why did the whale cross the ocean?

To get to the other tide

182) What's so special about bullets?

They're the only things that do their job after they're fired!

183) What does a pig use when he gets a cut?

Oinkment!

184) What does a cloud wear under his raincoat?

Thunderwear.

185) What do porcupines say when they kiss?

Ouch.

186) What do cows read?

CATTLE-logs.

187) What did the volcano say to his wife?

"I lava you so much."

188) Why are Teddy Bears never hungry?

Because they are always stuffed.

189) What do you give a sick lemon?

Lemon aid.

190) What animal needs oil?

A mouse because it squeaks.

191) What has three letters and starts with gas?

A car.

192) What did the blanket say to the bed?

I've got you covered.

193) What has two legs but can't walk?

A pair of pants.

194) What do you call a dog on the beach in summer?

A hot dog.

195) Why did the little boy throw his clock out the window?

Because he wanted to see time fly.

196) What did the stamp say to the envelope?

Stick with me, and we'll go places together.

197) Why can't the chicken cross the road?

Because he is too chicken

198) What did the football coach say to the broken vending machine?

I want my quarterback

199) What did the finger say to the thumb?

I'm in glove with you!

200) What is invisible and smells like carrots?

Rabbit farts

ABOUT THE AUTHOR

AUTHOR NAME is RUSTY COVE-SMITH

Find out more at http://amazon.com/author/rustycove

Or visit https://gimbooks.info/team/rusty-cove-smith/

MY OTHER BOOKS

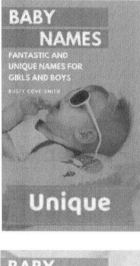

BABY NAMES:
FANTASTIC AND
UNIQUE NAMES FOR
GIRLS AND BOYS

Get it on Amazon!

BABY FOOD:
HEALTHY RECIPES
FOR BABIES AND
TODDLERS

Get it on Amazon!

CAN I ASK A FAVOR?

If you enjoyed this book, found it useful or otherwise, then I'd appreciate it if you would post a short review on Amazon. I do read all the reviews personally so that I can continually write what people are wanting.

If you'd like to leave a review, then please visit the link where you ordered this book from.

https://gimbooks.info/review-riddles/

Thanks for your support!

PLEASE REVIEW THE BOOK

Rusty Cove Smith

46927568R10106

Made in the USA
Middletown, DE
03 June 2019